Fast Food:
Slowing Us All Down

Slim Goodbody's
LIGHTEN UP
SERIES

Crabtree Publishing Company
www.crabtreebooks.com

Series Development and Packaging: John Burstein, Slim Goodbody Corp.
Senior Script Development: Phoebe Backler
Managing Editor: Valerie J. Weber
Designer and Illustrator: Ben McGinnis
Graphic Design Agency: Adventure Advertising
Instructional Designer: Alan Backler, Ph. D.
Content Consultant: Betty Hubbard, Ed. D., Certified Health Education Specialist
Project Editor: Reagan Miller

Library and Archives Canada Cataloguing in Publication

Burstein, John.
    Fast food : slowing us all down / Slim Goodbody.

(Slim Goodbody's lighten up!)
ISBN 978-0-7787-3915-9 (bound).--ISBN 978-0-7787-3933-3 (pbk.)

    1. Convenience foods--Juvenile literature. 2. Food--Fat
content--Juvenile
literature. 3. Nutrition--Juvenile literature. 4. Fast food restaurants--
Juvenile
literature. I. Title. II. Series: Goodbody, Slim. Slim Goodbody's
lighten up!
RA784.G665 2008   j613.2
C2008-900730-1

Library of Congress Cataloging-in-Publication Data

Burstein, John.
    Fast food : slowing us all down / John Burstein.
      p. cm. -- (Slim Goodbody's lighten up!)
    Includes index.
    ISBN-13: 978-0-7787-3915-9 (rlb)
    ISBN-10: 0-7787-3915-5 (rlb)
    ISBN-13: 978-0-7787-3933-3 (pb)
    ISBN-10: 0-7787-3933-3 (pb)
    1. Nutrition--Juvenile literature. 2. Fast food restaurants--Juvenile
literature. 3. Convenience foods--Juvenile literature. I. Title.
    RJ206.B877 2008
    618.92--dc22
                           2008003585

Crabtree Publishing Company

www.crabtreebooks.com   1-800-387-7650

Published in Canada
Crabtree Publishing
616 Welland Ave.
St. Catharines, Ontario
L2M 5V6

Published in the United States
Crabtree Publishing
PMB16A
350 Fifth Ave., Suite 3308
New York, NY 10118

Published in the United Kingdom
Crabtree Publishing
White Cross Mills
High Town, Lancaster
LA1 4XS

Published in Australia
Crabtree Publishing
386 Mt. Alexander Rd.
Ascot Vale (Melbourne)
VIC 3032

Printed in the U.S.A.

TABLE OF CONTENTS

Slim Goodbody's
LIGHTEN UP
SERIES

HELLO THERE. I'M SLIM GOODBODY,

and my greatest goal in life is to help young people across the planet become healthy and active. After all, one in three kids in the United States is overweight. Without changing their eating and exercise habits, many of these young people will become overweight adults. They risk many possible health problems like **high blood pressure** or **diabetes.**

Today, I would like to introduce you to my friend Nick. Nick and his friend Evan want to buy new cell phones. They started working after school at the fast-food restaurant, Royal Burger, to earn money for the phones. Join Nick and Evan as they learn about the problems with eating too much fast food and discover how to take care of their bodies by making smart decisions about food.

FACTS ABOUT FAST FOOD

Hi, my name is Nick. Ever since I was a kid, I've loved the burgers and French fries at Royal Burger. When my friend Evan and I decided to get jobs so that we could save enough money to buy new cell phones, I suggested that we work at Royal Burger.

"Just think about it! We can eat all the fast food we want and save money for our cell phones at the same time!" I said excitedly.

"I don't know, man. If we eat fast food every day, we're going to get fat! I've got a reputation to keep," said Evan, flexing his arm muscles.

Slim Goodbody Says: Fast food is usually high in **calories**, sugar, **sodium,** and fat but low in important vitamins and minerals. It is easy to eat all of the fat and calories that you need in a day in just one fast-food meal. Unfortunately, on average, children between the ages of eleven and eighteen eat at fast-food restaurants twice a week!

"Come on, it'll be great," I said. "Royal Burger has new healthier foods too, like salads and fruit plates. You can eat those if you're so worried about how you look."

Slim Goodbody Says: If you ask, most fast-food restaurants can give you **Nutrition Facts labels** and ingredient lists that can help you make healthier choices about what you eat. Their websites are also good places to look for nutritional information.

"Hey, it isn't just that I don't want to get fat. I don't want to eat too much fast food and wind up with high blood pressure and heart disease," said Evan.

THE BUDDY SYSTEM

"Listen, we can just look out for each other. If you're eating too much fast food, I'll let you know," I said.

"All right, I'll try it for a few months and see how it goes," said Evan.

KNOWING ABOUT NUTRITION

The next week, Evan and I were in health class, listening to Mrs. Morris, our health teacher.

"I want to start class with a discussion about fast food. How many of you eat fast food at least twice a month?" asked Mrs. Morris. Most of the kids in our class raised their hands.

"Well, you should know that most fast foods are high in sodium, which can lead to high blood pressure. They are also often high in **saturated fats** and **trans fats**. Does anyone know why it's a bad idea to eat foods with saturated and trans fats?" asked Mrs. Morris.

Casey, one of the girls in our class, raised her hand. "I read that they can raise your blood **cholesterol** levels and put you at a higher risk for heart disease, **strokes**, diabetes, and some types of cancer."

"That's right. At the same time, fast food is generally low in **fiber** and other important **nutrients** like vitamins A and C," said Mrs. Morris.

"Come on, Mrs. M. Are you telling us we should stop eating fast food altogether?" whined Sam, one of the kids in our class.

LEARN FROM THE LABEL

"I'm not saying that, but you should be mindful of the food that you eat. Before you order, ask for the Nutrition Facts label for the food you want. The Nutrition Facts label shows the percentage of nutrients in each serving of food. So if one serving has 25 percent of fat, it means that it contains one-fourth of the fat that you need in a day if you eat a typical 2000-calorie diet," explained Mrs. Morris.

Mrs. Morris continued, "I want you to look at these two Nutrition Facts labels and decide which of these foods are healthier. This nutrition chart will help you decide if these foods are low, moderate, or high in different nutrients."

You Should	Limit bad nutrients like fat, saturated fat, and sodium	Eat more good nutrients like **calcium**, vitamin A, and vitamin C	Look for foods that are low in calories
Healthy	5 percent or less of bad nutrients is LOW	20 percent or more of good nutrients is HIGH	100 calories per serving or below is LOW
Less Healthy	5 to 20 percent is MODERATE	5 to 20 percent is MODERATE	100 to 400 calories per serving is MODERATE
Unhealthy	20 percent or more is HIGH	5 percent or less is LOW	400 calories and above per serving is HIGH

Slim Goodbody Says: It is important to remember that not all of the nutrient totals in a food will fit perfectly into these ranges for healthy, less healthy, and unhealthy foods. Be a careful judge; look to see if a food is basically low in fat, calories, and sodium and make sure it has a healthy amount of fiber and some vitamins and minerals.

Salad with Grilled Chicken and Low-Fat Dressing

(Note: This label assumes that you will eat the dressing with your salad. The nutrient measurements include both the vegetables in the salad as well as the low-fat dressing

Nutrition Facts

Serving Size 12.3 oz./1.5 fluid oz. 350g/44ml   Servings Per Container 1

Amount Per Serving

Calories 360   Calories from Fat 115

	% Daily Value*
Total Fat 12g	19%
Saturated Fat 3g	14%
Trans Fat 0g	
Cholesterol 70mg	24%
Sodium 1700mg	70%
Total Carbohydrates 34g	11%
Dietary Fiber 7g	27%
Sugars 14g	
Protein 30g	

Vitamin A 130%	•	Vitamin C 54%
Calcium 15%	•	Iron 15%

*Percent Daily Values are based on a 2,000 calorie diet. Your daily values may be higher or lower depending on your calorie needs.

Chrispy Chicken Club Sandwich

Nutrition Facts

Serving Size 9.3 oz. (263g) Servings Per Container 1

Amount Per Serving

Calories 660   Calories from Fat 250

	% Daily Value*
Total Fat 28g	43%
Saturated Fat 8g	41%
Trans Fat 1.5g	
Cholesterol 80mg	27%
Sodium 1860mg	77%
Total Carbohydrates 63g	21%
Dietary Fiber 4g	14%
Sugars 11g	
Protein 39g	

Vitamin A 8%	•	Vitamin C 10%
Calcium 20%	•	Iron 20%

*Percent Daily Values are based on a 2,000 calorie diet. Your daily values may be higher or lower depending on your calorie needs.

Casey raised her hand again. "It looks like they are both high in sodium. The salad has a moderate amount of fat, but it's high in good nutrients like vitamin A. The chicken sandwich is high in saturated fat, and it has trans fat too."

"Exactly. You can see how these Nutrition Facts labels can give you useful information when you are choosing your meals," explained Mrs. Morris. "Remember, if you eat fast food for one meal, you need to make sure you eat healthy foods for your other meals."

Select Small Servings!

That afternoon, Evan and I arrived at Royal Burger for our first day of work. Roy, our manager, gave us our uniforms. We got right to work flipping burgers. A few hours later, Roy told us to take a break.

"I'm so hungry," Evan said. "But after listening to Mrs. Morris today, I don't think I want to eat any of this food."

I grabbed a double cheeseburger dripping with sauce and a massive container of French fries. "I saw the Nutrition Facts labels under the cash register. Use those to find your healthy food," I told him, and found a table where I could devour my meal.

What's in Your Food?

Evan walked over as I was polishing off the last of my fries.

"Man, you don't know what you're missing." I said looking at his single cheeseburger and small French fries.

"Yes I do. Sodium, saturated fat, and a whole lot of calories," said Evan. He handed me two Nutrition Facts labels for the fries.

Slim Goodbody Says: In general, it is healthier to eat smaller servings when you go to fast-food restaurants. The larger servings have more fat, sodium, and calories and they are still low in healthier nutrients like fiber, calcium, and vitamin A. Resist the urge to "super size" your meals. Super sizing can add up to 25 percent more fat and calories than the smaller serving.

Also, a single serving of meat is 2-3 ounces (57-85g), about the size of a deck of cards. Double hamburgers contain much more meat than this. Having too much meat in your diet can lead to health problems such as heart disease.

Take a look at these Nutrition Facts labels and answer these questions.
1. How many more calories are in the large fries than in the small fries?
2. How much more fat is in the large fries than in the small fries?
3. How much more sodium is in the large fries than in the small fries?

Small Fries

Nutrition Facts

Serving Size 2.6 oz. (74g)
Servings Per Container 1

Amount Per Serving	
Calories 250	Calories from Fat 120

	% Daily Value*
Total Fat 13g	**20%**
Saturated Fat 2.5g	13%
Trans Fat 3.5g	
Cholesterol 0mg	**0%**
Sodium 140mg	**6%**
Total Carbohydrates 30g	**10%**
Dietary Fiber 3g	12%
Sugars 0g	
Protein 2g	

Vitamin A 0%	•	Vitamin C 6%	
Calcium 2%		Iron 4%	

*Percent Daily Values are based on a 2,000 calorie diet. Your daily values may be higher or lower depending on your calorie needs.

Large Fries

Nutrition Facts

Serving Size 6 oz. (170g)
Servings Per Container 1

Amount Per Serving	
Calories 570	Calories from Fat 270

	% Daily Value*
Total Fat 30g	**47%**
Saturated Fat 6g	30%
Trans Fat 8g	
Cholesterol 0mg	**0%**
Sodium 330mg	**14%**
Total Carbohydrates 70g	**23%**
Dietary Fiber 7g	28%
Sugars 0g	
Protein 6g	

Vitamin A 0%	•	Vitamin C 15%	
Calcium 2%		Iron 10%	

*Percent Daily Values are based on a 2,000 calorie diet. Your daily values may be higher or lower depending on your calorie needs.

Answers:

1. You would cut 320 calories by eating the small fries.

2. The large fries have 27 percent more fat than the small fries.

3. They also have 8 percent more sodium

"All right," I said. "So my large fries had a lot of fat and sodium."

"And calories too, but if you think the fries are bad, look at these," said Evan, handing me the burger Nutrition Facts labels.

"Wow," I said in amazement. "I never realized how bad this food can be for your health!"

"Now you do," said Evan, shaking his head and laughing. "Your double cheeseburger is higher in calories and fat, including saturated fat and trans fat, and sodium than my single cheeseburger. You don't even get much more fiber, vitamin A, or any extra vitamin C."

Single Cheeseburger

Nutrition Facts

Serving Size 4 oz. (114g)
Servings Per Container 1

Amount Per Serving	
Calories 300	Calories from Fat 110

	% Daily Value*
Total Fat 12g	**19%**
Saturated Fat 6g	28%
Trans Fat 0.5g	
Cholesterol 40mg	**13%**
Sodium 750mg	**31%**
Total Carbohydrates 33g	**11%**
Dietary Fiber 2g	7%
Sugars 6g	
Protein 15g	

Vitamin A 6%	•	Vitamin C 2%	
Calcium 20%	•	Iron 15%	

*Percent Daily Values are based on a 2,000 calorie diet. Your daily values may be higher or lower depending on your calorie needs.

Double Cheeseburger

Nutrition Facts

Serving Size 5.8 oz. (165g)
Servings Per Container 1

Amount Per Serving	
Calories 440	Calories from Fat 210

	% Daily Value*
Total Fat 23g	**35%**
Saturated Fat 11g	54%
Trans Fat 1.5g	
Cholesterol 80mg	**26%**
Sodium 1150mg	**48%**
Total Carbohydrates 34g	**11%**
Dietary Fiber 2g	8%
Sugars 7g	
Protein 25g	

Vitamin A 10%	•	Vitamin C 2%	
Calcium 25%	•	Iron 20%	

*Percent Daily Values are based on a 2,000 calorie diet. Your daily values may be higher or lower depending on your calorie needs.

THE DOWNSIDE OF SUGARY DRINKS

The next day after school, Evan and I walked to work under the blazing sun. As soon as we arrived at Royal Burger, I went to the ice cream machine and made myself a huge vanilla milkshake. It took me no time at all to drink the whole thing, and it was delicious.

"Nick, when are you going to learn?" said Evan, laughing at me. "Those shakes are the worst."

"Come on, they can't be that bad," I said, rolling my eyes.

THE MILKSHAKE MISHAP

"Oh yeah? Take a look at the number of calories in your milkshake," said Evan, handing me the Nutrition Facts label.

Thick Vanilla Shake

Nutrition Facts		
Serving Size	32 fluid oz. (888ml)	
Servings Per Container 1		

Amount Per Serving		
Calories 1110	Calories from Fat 240	
		% Daily Value*
Total Fat 26g		41%
Saturated Fat 16g		80%
Trans Fat 2g		
Cholesterol 100mg		34%
Sodium 370mg		16%
Total Carbohydrates 193g		64%
Dietary Fiber 0g		0%
Sugars 145g		
Protein 25g		

Vitamin A 40%	•	Vitamin C 0%
Calcium 90%	•	Iron 2%

*Percent Daily Values are based on a 2,000 calorie diet. Your daily values may be higher or lower depending on your calorie needs.

"Over 1,000 calories! I can't believe it! I just drank half the number of calories I'm supposed to eat in a whole day?" I asked in amazement.

"Looks like it," Evan replied.

Slim Goodbody Says: Foods and drinks with a lot of sugar are high in calories and low in healthy nutrients. Look for foods and beverages low in added sweeteners. The ingredients list can help you make the smart choice. If added sweeteners are listed in the first few ingredients, choose another drink. Some names for added sweeteners include sucrose, glucose, dextrose, high-fructose corn syrup, corn syrup, maple syrup, lactose, and fructose.

Take a look at this ingredients list for a 12-ounce (355 ml) vanilla triple-thick shake. Does it look like a healthy choice to you?

Vanilla Reduced Fat Ice Cream: Milk, sugar, cream, nonfat milk solids, corn syrup solids, mono- and diglycerides, guar gum, dextrose, sodium citrate, artificial vanilla flavor, sodium phosphate, carrageenan, disodium phosphate, cellulose gum, vitamin A palmitate. CONTAINS: MILK. Vanilla Syrup: Corn syrup, water, natural flavor, caramel color, citric acid, pectin, sodium benzoate, yellow 5, yellow 6.

"All right, you win. Next time I'll just have a soda," I said, throwing my cup in the trash can.

"You know, even sodas are high in sugar and calories," said Evan.

"So what can I do? I've got to drink something!" I said.

Ethan tossed me a bottle of water and said, "The best thing to do is to drink water. It doesn't have any calories, and your body needs it in order to stay **hydrated**."

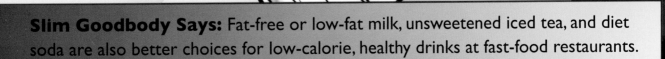

Slim Goodbody Says: Fat-free or low-fat milk, unsweetened iced tea, and diet soda are also better choices for low-calorie, healthy drinks at fast-food restaurants.

HAVE A HEALTHIER SIDE DISH

Later that day, Roy told us we could take a break. After my vanilla milkshake, I decided to find something healthy to go with my hamburger. I looked in the cooler at the different Royal Burger salads.

"Now you're thinking straight," Evan said.

I nodded my head and took a salad from the cooler along with a package of low-fat dressing.

Slim Goodbody Says: This salad dressing maybe low in fat, but watch out for sodium. Low-fat dressings often use a lot of sodium to add flavor. If you order a low-fat dressing, just use half the package to keep the meal healthy.

As I sat down, I saw Evan coming to the table with his cheeseburger and a small container of fries.

"Finally I'm the one making healthy choices around here!" I said, pointing at his fries and smirking.

"You've got me on this one. Your salad is way healthier than my fries. I don't even need to look at the Nutrition Facts label to know that it's got fewer calories, fat, and sodium," said Evan, smiling. "Of course, I'm not the one that drank the world's largest milkshake earlier today!"

12

BALANCE IS BEST

"Good point," I grinned. "I guess it's just like Mrs. Morris said. If you eat fast food for one meal, you really should eat healthy foods for the rest of the day."

"Yeah, It's all about balance," agreed Evan.

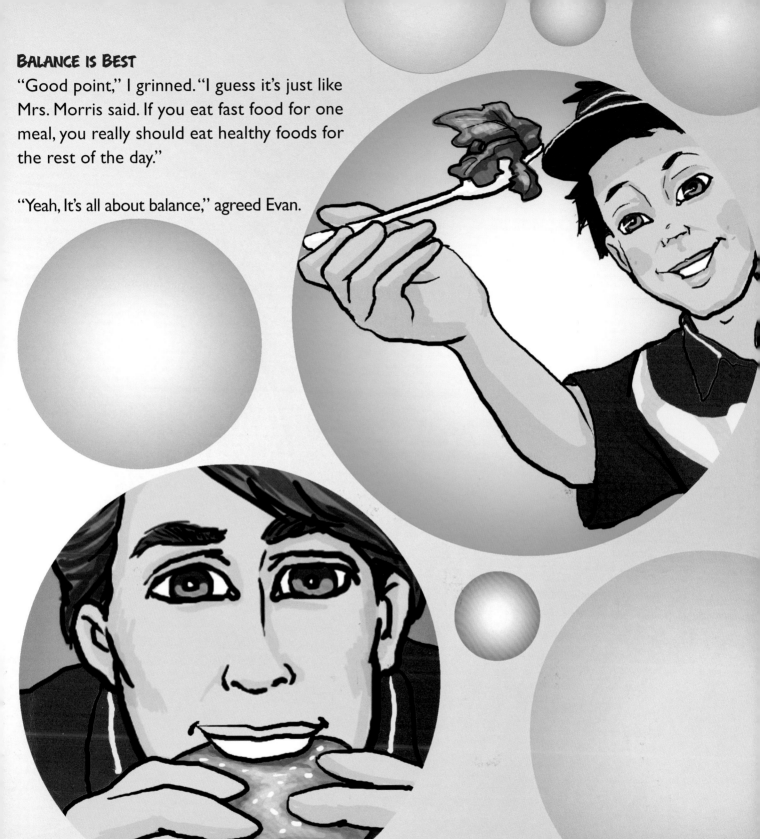

 **Slim Goodbody Says:** Fast-food restaurants are getting better about offering healthy side dishes such as salads and fruits. Make sure that you are getting important nutrients. Instead of ordering fries or onion rings with your meal, try baked potato chips, a fruit and yogurt bowl, or a side salad.

SKIP THE SAUCE

A few weeks later, I noticed that some of my clothes seemed to fit a little tightly. Even though I was trying to eat some salads at Royal Burger, it was obvious that I was starting to gain weight from eating so much fast food. My skin was also starting to break out with acne, and I felt tired all the time. That afternoon at work, I asked Evan if he was noticing any difference from eating so much fast food.

"Not really, but I'm exercising more and trying to be really careful about what I eat at work," said Evan. "When you eat your hamburgers, do you get the special sauce and mayonnaise on them?"

"Of course! The special sauce is what makes the burgers taste so good," I said.

THE DANGERS OF SAUCES

"That's part of your problem. Those sauces are really high in fat and calories. I've been getting the reduced-fat mayonnaise or else just eating the burgers plain," explained Evan. "When you get bacon on your cheeseburger, it's the same problem. Bacon is bad news. It's got a lot of fat and calories."

Slim Goodbody Says: At other fast-food restaurants, you might see unhealthy **condiments** like cheese sauce, tartar sauce, sour cream, gravy, and guacamole. Those sauces are all high in calories and fat. Try ordering pickles, onions, lettuce, tomatoes, mustard, and ketchup on your sandwich to add flavor without the fat. At a Mexican fast-food restaurant, ask for salsa with your meal instead of nacho cheese sauce.

"All right, all right! I'll quit eating the sauces. I guess it's worth it. I don't want to have to go out and buy bigger clothes," I told Evan.

Slim Goodbody Says: Take a look at these two Nutrition Facts labels. Compare the chicken with sauce to the chicken without sauce and answer these questions:

1. How many more calories are in the chicken with sauce than the chicken without sauce?
2. How much more total fat is in the chicken with sauce?
3. How much less saturated fat is in the chicken without sauce?

Roasted Chicken with Sauce

Nutrition Facts
Serving Size 7.4 oz. (211g)
Servings Per Container 1

Amount Per Serving	
Calories 350	Calories from Fat 130

	% Daily Value*
Total Fat 15g	23%
Saturated Fat 3g	15%
Trans Fat 0g	
Cholesterol 75mg	25%
Sodium 880mg	37%
Total Carbohydrates 23g	8%
Dietary Fiber 1g	4%
Sugars 1g	
Protein 32g	

Vitamin A 4%	•	Vitamin C <2%
Calcium 4%	•	Iron 10%

*Percent Daily Values are based on a 2,000 calorie diet. Your daily values may be higher or lower depending on your calorie needs.

Roasted Chicken without Sauce

Nutrition Facts
Serving Size 6.2 oz. (177g)
Servings Per Container 1

Amount Per Serving	
Calories 270	Calories from Fat 45

	% Daily Value*
Total Fat 5g	8%
Saturated Fat 1.5g	8%
Trans Fat 0g	
Cholesterol 65mg	22%
Sodium 690mg	29%
Total Carbohydrates 26g	9%
Dietary Fiber 1g	4%
Sugars <1g	
Protein 31g	

Vitamin A <2%	•	Vitamin C <2%
Calcium 4%	•	Iron 10%

*Percent Daily Values are based on a 2,000 calorie diet. Your daily values may be higher or lower depending on your calorie needs.

Answers: 1. 80 calories 2. 10 grams 3. 1.5 grams or half the saturated fat

15

Go for the Grilled!

The next day, Evan and I had the day off from work. After school, we decided to work out at the school's gym. The gym teacher, Ms. Austin, was setting up a new workout machine when we arrived.

"Hey, Ms. Austin, mind if we lift some weights?" asked Evan.

"Come on in, guys. I haven't seen you two around much these days. What have you been up to?" she asked.

The Burger Bulge

"We started working at Royal Burger," I told her. "And I'm afraid all those burgers are starting to show," I said, patting my stomach's new bulge.

"Yes, you really have to pay attention to what you order in those fast-food restaurants," said Ms. Austin.

"Tell me about it. I had a 1000-calorie milkshake the other day!"

"The fried sandwiches are pretty bad too," said Ms. Austin. "I used to get the crispy chicken sandwiches when I ate fast food. Chicken has less fat than beef. But adding batter and deep-frying chicken adds a lot of saturated and trans fats. I try not to eat much fast food anymore, but when I do, I get the grilled chicken."

SHOULDERS TO SHINS
ATHLETIC EQUIPMENT

Slim Goodbody Says: Ms. Austin is right; fried fish sandwiches and chicken nuggets are high in calories and saturated fat. If you are going to eat fast food, look for lean meats like chicken and fish that are grilled.

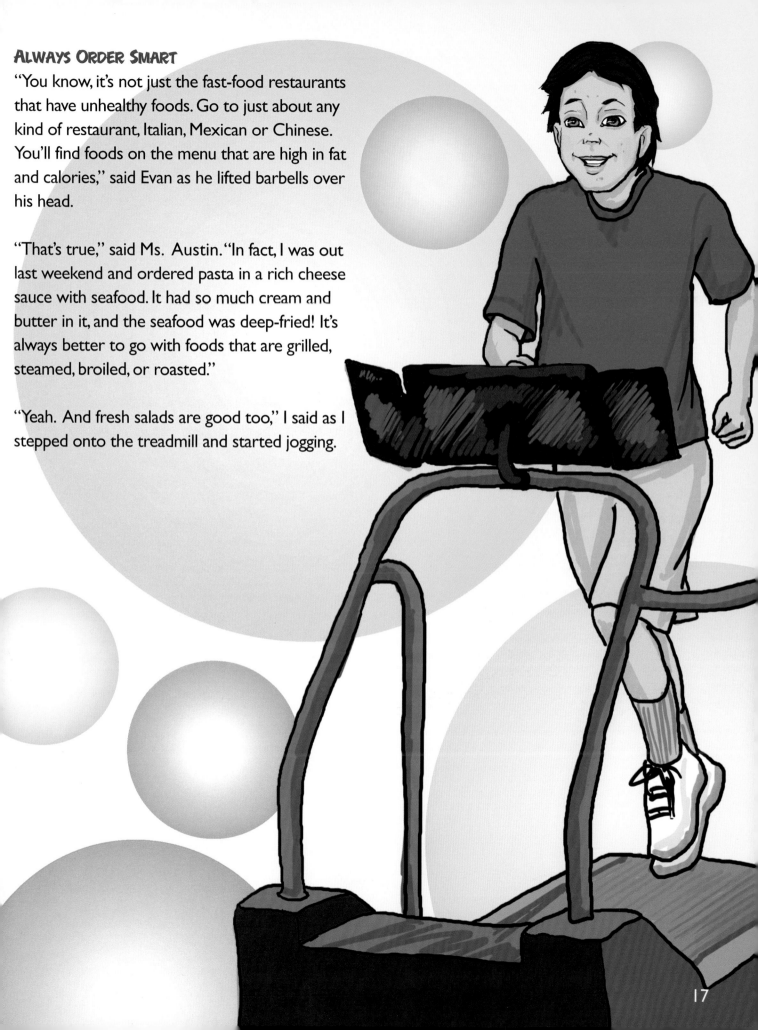

ALWAYS ORDER SMART

"You know, it's not just the fast-food restaurants that have unhealthy foods. Go to just about any kind of restaurant, Italian, Mexican or Chinese. You'll find foods on the menu that are high in fat and calories," said Evan as he lifted barbells over his head.

"That's true," said Ms. Austin. "In fact, I was out last weekend and ordered pasta in a rich cheese sauce with seafood. It had so much cream and butter in it, and the seafood was deep-fried! It's always better to go with foods that are grilled, steamed, broiled, or roasted."

"Yeah. And fresh salads are good too," I said as I stepped onto the treadmill and started jogging.

HEALTHY DECISIONS FOR A HEALTHY LIFE

"My problem is that when I have the choice between a juicy burger and a salad, I can never convince myself to eat the salad," I admitted.

"It can be hard to make healthy decisions, but it is a useful skill to develop now," Ms. Austin told me. "You have to make choices about what you eat all your life. If you start learning how to stick to the nutritious foods now, you'll have a much better chance of growing up into a healthy adult."

"I know you're right," I said.

THE FIVE STEPS TO HEALTHY DECISIONS

"I've got a little tool I use to help me with making decisions. Once I think about it, it's easier to choose the healthy food. First, you need to *identify your choices*. Then you *evaluate each choice* and *think about their consequences*. Then you *identify the healthiest decision* and *take action*. Afterward, it's helpful to think back and *evaluate your decision*. That way, you'll know if you made the right choice," explained Ms. Austin.

"That seems pretty clear. I'll give it a try," I said. "Thanks, Ms. Austin.

The next day at work when Roy gave us our break, I thought back to Ms. Austin's advice. I was really hungry. But before I grabbed a burger, I stopped myself. "OK, I can have a grilled chicken sandwich or a hamburger. The chicken has less fat, and if I eat the hamburger, I'll just gain more weight. I guess the healthiest choice is the grilled chicken sandwich," I thought to myself. "I'll even put lettuce and pickles on it instead of mayonnaise to give it extra flavor."
After I finished the sandwich, I wasn't hungry anymore, and I felt good about eating the healthier meal. "I know I made the right choice," I thought to myself.

Slim Goodbody Says: Now it's your turn to use Ms. Austin's decision-making tool. Now compare your choices in the menu below. What foods would you choose to have a healthy meal?

Drinks
- Milkshake
- 100% pure orange juice
- Fortified low-fat or fat-free milk
- Soft drink

Side Dishes
- French fries
- Baked potato with low-fat sour cream
- Onion rings
- Fruit and yogurt dish

Main Course
- Chicken nuggets
- Fried fish sandwich
- Grilled chicken
- Salad bar

Key: The healthy choices are:
Drinks
100% pure orange juice is high in vitamin C, and it is fat free.
or
Fortified low-fat or fat-free milk is high in vitamins A and D and calcium.

Side Dishes
A baked potato with low-fat sour cream is low in fat and high in vitamins and minerals.
or
Fruit and yogurt dishes are also high in vitamins and minerals and low in fat and calories.

Main Course
Grilled chicken is a healthy source of protein.
or
The salad bar offers a lot of vitamins and minerals.

Go for the Goal!

The next day in school, I found Ms. Austin before heading to work.

"Hey, I wanted to thank you for teaching me your decision-making tool. It's already helped," I told her.

"That's great, Nick. I was thinking that it would probably help if you set some goals too. I always have an easier time making healthy choices when I'm working toward a goal," said Ms. Austin.

"Yeah, you're probably right. I've never been very good at setting goals though," I admitted.

Setting Great Goals

"Well, you're in luck. I've got a helpful tool for setting goals too. It's pretty easy, really," she said. "First, *write down a realistic goal.* Then *list the steps you need to take to achieve that goal.*. Then *think about what kinds of help and support you will need from your friends and family to meet the goal.*. Finally you *evaluate your progress* and if you have reached your goal, you *reward yourself.* It is much easier to evaluate your progress if you set your goal for a certain amount of time like two weeks or a month," Ms. Austin suggested.

"That sounds easy enough," I said and thought for a while. "I guess my goal is to order healthy foods when I am eating out for the next two weeks. To do that, I'll look on the menu for foods that are grilled and for fresh vegetables and fruits."

20

"That's great, Nick," said Ms. Austin encouragingly. "Now, what kinds of support will you need from your friends and family to reach your goal?"

"Well, Evan is already pretty good at pointing out when I am eating unhealthy foods. I can also let my parents know about my goal. They can remind me to look for healthy foods when we go out," I told her.

"All right, and if you eat well when you go out for the next two weeks, how will you reward yourself?" asked Ms. Austin.

"Hmm, maybe I'll go online and get a ring tone for the new cell phone I'm going to buy," I said.

"That sounds like a great plan," said Ms. Austin.

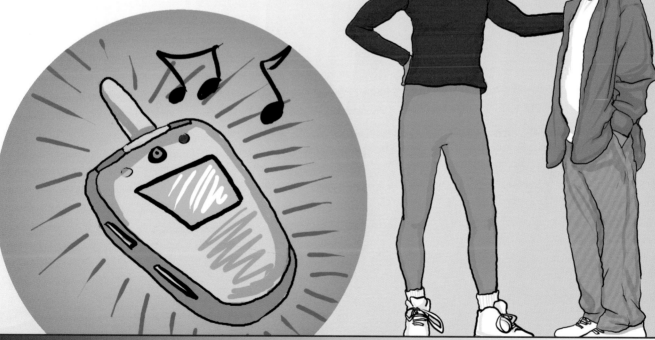

Slim Goodbody Says: Now it's your turn to use Ms. Austin's goal-setting tool and set your own healthy goals for eating at fast-food restaurants. Remember, learning how to set healthy goals and following through with them is an important skill that you will be able to use for the rest of your life. What will your goal be?

Using Refusal Skills

"The only problem with this plan is that Evan is my only friend who cares about eating well. My other friends always make fun of Evan when he eats salads instead of burgers," I said.

"He doesn't seem to mind," Ms. Austin observed.

"No, but Evan is different. Everyone thinks he's cool. I just can't imagine going out with friends and ordering a grilled chicken salad," I laughed.

"Well, now that you've set a goal, it may be easier to use **refusal skills** and say no to something you don't want. Imagine you are at a fast-food restaurant with your buddies. They are all getting super-sized meals. They ask you what you're going to order. You say that you're getting a grilled chicken salad. They tease you, 'Are you crazy? Come on, get a burger with us.'"

"Yeah, that sounds about right," I said.

How to Say No to Unhealthy Choices

"It can be hard to do, especially with your friends, but the process is simple. You say 'No' in a firm voice. Then explain to your friends why you would rather eat your salad. If they still give you a hard time, you can offer other options, like 'Let's go to the sandwich shop next door where there are more choices. That way we can all find something we want to eat,'" Ms. Austin advised me.

"And what if they still make fun of me?" I asked.

"Well, you can simply walk away. If they're real friends, they'll get the message and lay off in the future. Who knows, you may even convince your friends to pass on the fries and milkshakes!" said Ms. Austin.

SAY NO!
EXPLAIN WHY...
OFFER OPTIONS!
WALK AWAY.

 **Slim Goodbody Says:** Do your friends ever pressure you to make unhealthy choices? Learning how to say no to unhealthy situations is a very important skill to develop.

HEROES OF HEALTH ADVOCACY

The next week, Evan and I were back in health class. Our health teacher, Mrs. Morris, began a new presentation.

"I want to talk with you today about becoming a **health advocate**." said Mrs. Morris.

"What's that?" asked Casey.

"A health advocate is someone who educates their family and community about making healthy choices. My nephew, Edward, is a perfect example. Ed struggled for a long time with his weight. He had such a busy schedule between school, football practice, and playing saxophone in the school band that he didn't have time to think much about what he ate. He would stop at a fast-food restaurant for breakfast on his way to school and then again after football practice. You can imagine what eating fast food two or three times a day did to his health. He gained a lot of weight and started feeling sick. Finally, he went to the doctor who told Ed that he was putting his heart at risk by eating so much unhealthy food."

"Wow," said Casey. "So what did he do?"

BE A HEALTH ADVOCATE

LEARNING FROM MISTAKES

"Well, Ed and his doctor came up with a plan for a healthy diet. Ed stopped going to fast-food restaurants and made sure that he ate balanced meals with plenty of fruits, vegetables, and **whole grains**. He also started running every day after school since football season was over," said Mrs. Morris. "Now he looks like a new kid.

He is fit, healthy, and full of energy. He decided to use his experience to teach other teenagers about the importance of eating well. He started volunteering with the American Heart Association. He gives speeches at schools, telling his story and giving advice to kids who need help making healthier choices."

 **Slim Goodbody Says:** Your doctor can be a helpful partner in designing a new health plan for your life too. Talk with your doctor if you want to work on becoming more fit and healthy. Your health teacher, school nurse, or the health director at a local teen club can all be great resources too.

BE A HEALTH ADVOCATE
- take a healthy stand on an issue
- persuade others to make a healthy choice
- be convincing

"That's pretty cool," I said. "Why don't we have any health advocates at our school?"

"All of you can be health advocates!" replied Mrs. Morris. "All you have to do is *take a healthy stand on an issue.* Then you have to *persuade others to make a healthy choice,* and you need to *be convincing.*"

TEACH OTHERS: BECOME A HEALTH ADVOCATE

A few weeks later, my skin had cleared up, and all my old clothes fit again. I'd been working out with Evan and paying a lot more attention to what I ate. That evening, my mother took me out to eat at my favorite Mexican restaurant.

"I think I'll have a taco salad," my mother said as she read the menu.

"You know, Mom, taco salads aren't very healthy," I said. "They come in deep-fried shells that are really high in fat."

"I always think of salads as a health food," said my mother with surprise.

"You can always get the salad without the shell," I suggested. I went to the counter to ask for a Nutrition Facts label and then shared the information with my mother.

Slim Goodbody Says: Compare the fat, calories, and sodium in the taco salad with a shell to the taco salad without a shell.

Taco Salad with Shell

Nutrition Facts

Serving Size	548g
Servings Per Container 1	

Amount Per Serving

Calories 840	Calories from Fat 400

	% Daily Value*
Total Fat 24g	69%
Saturated Fat 11g	55%
Trans Fat 1.5g	
Cholesterol 65mg	22%
Sodium 1780mg	74%
Total Carbohydrates 80g	27%
Dietary Fiber 15g	60%
Sugars 10g	
Protein 30g	

Vitamin A 25%	•	Vitamin C 20%
Calcium 45%	•	Iron 40%

*Percent Daily Values are based on a 2,000 calorie diet. Your daily values may be higher or lower depending on your calorie needs.

Taco Salad without Shell

Nutrition Facts

Serving Size	479g
Servings Per Container 1	

Amount Per Serving

Calories 470	Calories from Fat 220

	% Daily Value*
Total Fat 24g	27%
Saturated Fat 10g	50%
Trans Fat 1.5g	
Cholesterol 65mg	22%
Sodium 1510mg	63%
Total Carbohydrates 41g	14%
Dietary Fiber 13g	52%
Sugars 9g	
Protein 23g	

Vitamin A 25%	•	Vitamin C 20%
Calcium 30%	•	Iron 25%

*Percent Daily Values are based on a 2,000 calorie diet. Your daily values may be higher or lower depending on your calorie needs.

"See, the shell adds 370 calories and increases the total fat and the sodium," I explained. "The truth is neither of these salads is very healthy. Maybe you can get a green salad or a bean burrito instead."

NICK BECOMES A HEALTH ADVOCATE

"I never thought that you'd be educating me about healthy eating, Nick! Since when do you know so much about nutrition?" asked my mother.

"I learned a lot from working at Royal Burger and in health class. Mrs. Morris also told us about health advocates. They teach their friends and families how to work toward healthier lifestyles," I said. "She explained to us that health advocates take a healthy stand on an issue. Then they persuade others to make healthy choices, and they are convincing. I want to teach people how to choose healthy foods. Now I know enough about **nutrition** to do it. Plus, I can use my own experience of learning from my mistakes to be convincing."

"You know, your friends at school eat a lot of junk food. Maybe you should start with them. If they learn healthy habits now, they'll have a much better chance of growing up into healthy adults," suggested my mother.

"That's not a bad idea," I told her. "Maybe I'll give it a try!"

Slim Goodbody Says: Now it's your turn to become a health advocate. Talk with your health teacher about volunteer opportunities in your town. Maybe there is a walk-a-thon to raise money and awareness for a health organization like the American Heart Association. Get your friends and family to join you and have fun being active and spreading a healthy message together!

THE ROYAL BURGER WRAP-UP

A week later, I was out with my friends. We were all hungry and decided to get something to eat.

"Let's go to Royal Burger," suggested Allan.

At the counter, my friends ordered value meals. Evan and I asked for a grilled chicken salad.

"Salads!" laughed Sam. "What, are you guys on a diet?"

HELPING FRIENDS MAKE HEALTHY CHOICES

"Listen, I've learned from experience that if I eat too much junk food, my skin breaks out and I get fat. I'm done with feeling unhealthy and tired all the time," I said. "Your super-sized fries have a ton of fat, calories, and sodium. You should be getting a small fries or even better a side salad or fruit plate."

"Yeah," said Evan. "You should probably get the grilled chicken instead of the deep-fried chicken sandwiches too. The grilled chicken is lower in fat. That extra sauce on your burger is also pretty bad. It's got all sorts of saturated fat and calories.

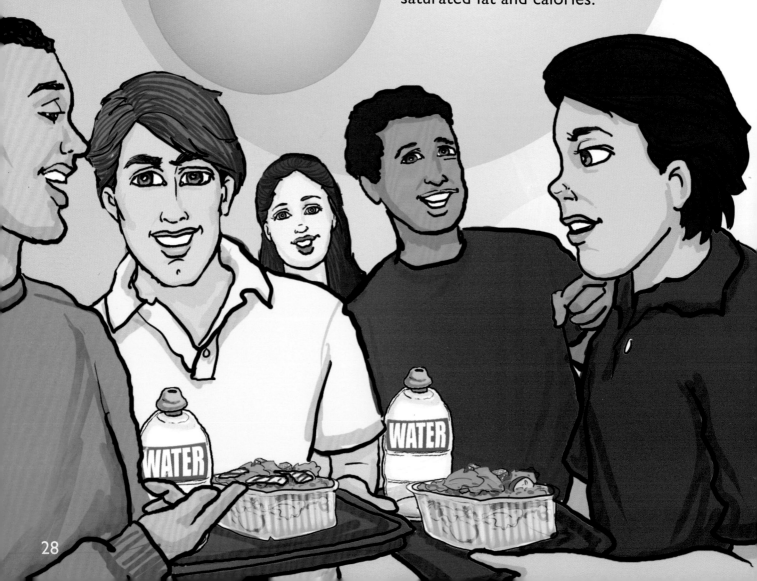

"What's wrong with you, Nick?" asked Allan. "I expect these lectures from Evan, but you're a freak about fast food. You used to eat more of it than the rest of us."

"I'm trying to tell you that I've learned from my mistakes. I don't want to have heart problems or diabetes when I get older. I've been setting goals to eat healthier, and it's made a big difference.

It's not always easy to make healthy choices, but I'm working on it. And I feel way better now. You guys should try it," I encouraged.

"It must be all that talk about health advocates in health class," said Allan.

"That's part of it," I admitted. "It's helped me to live a healthier lifestyle, so I figure it will help others too."

"All right, you guys. I'll give it a try. Next time we go out, you guys can order me a healthy meal. If it's any good, I'll think about eating better too," said Sam.

"You won't regret it, Sam," said Evan.

I felt great. I never thought I would be the one to convince my buddies to eat well. I guess working at Royal Burger really did make me a health advocate.

Slim Goodbody Says: Create a small poster listing all of the healthy eating tips that you have learned in this book. Keep your poster in the car. That way you and your family will be reminded to make healthy choices when you go out to eat!

GLOSSARY

calcium A mineral found in milk and other foods that helps the body build strong bones and teeth

calories Units of energy contained in foods and drinks. Calories are used to produce energy. Extra calories not used as energy may be stored as fat.

cholesterol A fatty substance found in animal products. Meats, egg yolks, and dairy products, such as butter and cheese, contain cholesterol.

condiments Sauces, relishes, or spices used to make food more flavorful

diabetes A disease in which people have too much sugar in their blood. People with diabetes cannot produce enough insulin, the substance the body needs to use sugar properly.

fiber Material in food that cannot be digested but helps with going to the bathroom

health advocate A person who works for a healthy cause

high blood pressure A condition that forces the heart to work harder to pump blood

hydrated Having enough water in the body

nutrients Chemical compounds (such as proteins, fats, carbohydrates, vitamins, or minerals) that make up foods. The body uses nutrients to function and grow.

nutrition The study of food and diet

Nutrition Facts labels Labels on the back of packaged foods that list the amount of nutrients in the food. The information in the Nutrition Facts label is based on a 2,000-calorie diet.

refusal skills The ability to say no to unhealthy choices in all situations

saturated fats Fats that tend to be solid at room temperature. They are usually found in animal products, such as beef, butter, and whole-fat milk, and can cause heart problems and high blood pressure.

sodium Salt, which can cause high blood pressure

strokes Losses of mental functions caused by broken blood vessels to the brain

trans fats Forms of fats found in solid fats, such as stick margarine and vegetable shortening, and in some processed foods. Trans fats improve the flavor and texture of foods, but they increase the risk of heart disease.

whole grains Foods with all three parts of a grain — the bran, the endosperm, and the germ. Whole grains have more fiber and nutrients than more refined grains.

FOR MORE INFORMATION

American Heart Association

www.americanheart.org/presenter.jhtml?identifier=3003754

Find fun ways you and your friends can raise money for the American Heart Association.

Center for Disease Control: BAM Body and Mind Website

www.bam.gov/sub_foodnutrition/index.html

Learn interesting facts and play games about nutrition and making healthy choices about the foods that you eat.

Center for Disease Control: BAM Body and Mind Website

www.bam.gov/sub_yourlife/yourlife_choices_3.html

This website explores the challenges of peer pressure. Learning to make healthy choices about the food you eat—and about saying "no" to cigarettes, drugs and alcohol—is a very important life skill. This website will help you learn how deal with peer pressure and to say no to unhealthy situations.

Family Education

life.familyeducation.com/nutrition/health/36613.html

Learn more about reading and interpreting Nutrition Facts labels.

Smart-Mouth

www.cspinet.org/smartmouth

This site explores the different tricks fast-food restaurants use to get people to buy unhealthy foods. Learn helpful tips for eating well and being more physically active.

United States Food and Drug Administration: Food Labeling and Nutrition

vm.cfsan.fda.gov/label.html

Learn more about Nutrition Facts labels and test your label knowledge with a quiz. This site also offers a basic brochure on food labels.

INDEX

ABOUT THE AUTHOR

John Burstein (also known as Slim Goodbody) has been entertaining and educating children for over thirty years. His programs have been broadcast on CBS, PBS, Nickelodeon, USA, and Discovery. He has won numerous awards including the Parent's Choice Award and the President's Council's Fitness Leader Award. Currently, Mr. Burstein tours the country with his live multimedia show "Bodyology." For more information, please visit slimgoodbody.com